Fun-to-Wear
Fabric Flowers

Elizabeth Helene Searle

LARK BOOKS

A Division of Sterling Publishing Co., Inc.

New York

DEVELOPMENT EDITOR: Valerie Shrader
ART DIRECTOR: Dana Irwin
COVER DESIGNER: Barbara Zaretsky
LINE EDITOR: McKenna Linn
ASSISTANT EDITOR: Rebecca Guthrie
ASSOCIATE EDITOR: Nathalie Mornu
ASSISTANT ART DIRECTOR: Lance Wille
ART PRODUCTION ASSISTANT: Jeff Hamilton
EDITORIAL ASSISTANCE: Delores Gosnell
EDITORIAL INTERN: David L. Squires
ART INTERN: Ardyce E. Alspach
PHOTOGRAPHER: John Widman
ILLUSTRATOR: Bernadette Wolf

10 9 8 7 6 5 4 3 2 1

First Edition

Published by Lark Books, A Division of
Sterling Publishing Co., Inc.
387 Park Avenue South, New York, N.Y. 10016

Text © 2006, Elizabeth Helene Searle
Photography © 2006, Lark Books
Illustrations © 2006, Lark Books

Distributed in Canada by Sterling Publishing,
c/o Canadian Manda Group, 165 Dufferin Street
Toronto, Ontario, Canada M6K 3H6

Distributed in the United Kingdom by GMC Distribution Services,
Castle Place, 166 High Street, Lewes, East Sussex, England BN7 1XU

Distributed in Australia by Capricorn Link (Australia) Pty Ltd.,
P.O. Box 704, Windsor, NSW 2756 Australia

If you have questions or comments about this book, please contact:
Lark Books
67 Broadway
Asheville, NC 28801
(828) 253-0467

Manufactured in China

ISBN 13: 978-1-57990-769-3
ISBN 1-57990-769-5

For information about custom editions, special sales, premium and corporate purchases, please
contact Sterling Special Sales Department at 800-805-5489 or specialsales@sterlingpub.com.

Fun-to-Wear
Fabric
Flowers

Contents

Introduction

I was born with a needle and thread in my hand. I know this because my grandmother told me I used to sew in my crib, and grandmothers never lie. Since then, not a day has gone by that I don't sew at least a stitch or two. My grandmother showed me how to thread a needle. She and my mother taught me a few basic stitches, and with that I was off and running on my lifelong adventure with fabric.

My introduction to making fabric flowers came over a decade ago when I was asked to teach a class. Since I could find no books on the subject, I just had to figure it out. I was in my element! I love the thrill of creating things with my hands using fabric, needle, and thread—the thrill of figuring things out.

I started experimenting with ribbon, but found that too limiting: never the right color and a narrow range of widths, weaves, and textures. But making flowers out of fabric opened a whole world of creative possibilities.

Since that first class, I've made thousands of fabric flowers and leaves, experimenting with materials and techniques in every way I could imagine. This book contains much of what I learned along the way. My hope is that by sharing what I had to figure out by trial and error, you can immediately begin to make flowers that look great using the easiest methods possible.

In this book, I'll show you how to make 36 different flowers and six types of leaves. You can make them exactly according to the instructions, of course. But the real fun is in creating your own unique variations. For instance, fabric flowers can be made to look realistic or stylized (what I call fantasy flowers), and petals can be made into leaves and leaves into petals, just by changing colors, fabrics, and placement. I encourage you to consider these instructions as simply a guide for your own experimentation. Try all types of fabrics, vary dimensions, mix-and-match elements, find new objects to use as centers, add unique embellishments…the sky's the limit to what you can do with fabric flowers. Each flower takes just a minimum investment of time and fabric (most can be made from scraps you already have on hand), so you have virtually nothing to lose by experimenting. Have fun! Create! And best of all, no weeding is required!

Uses for fabric flowers abound. People have been crafting flowers from all sorts of materials for centuries—to decorate and enliven their homes, to celebrate important occasions, and as personal adornment. Fabric flowers are no exception. Pin them to hats, collars, lapels, purses, even shoes, to add distinctive flair to your look, whether that look is elegant or eclectic. Mass them on a gown or wedding dress to add a personal touch to an important occasion. Use them to create a centerpiece for your dining table, a unique wall hanging for your home, or a bow for a special gift.

Another big plus about fabric flowers is that you don't need a lot of fancy tools or equipment. Most of the projects in this book can be made entirely by hand. A sewing machine can be used to speed up some of the processes (such as gathering) and a serger can be used to add decorative edges, but neither is required. The actual construction of each flower is done by hand. This makes the projects portable, as well as quick and easy.

So what are you waiting for? The sooner you make your garden of fabric flowers, the sooner you can have fun wearing them!

Fabric Flower Basics

Whether realistic or fantastic, fabric flowers are easy to craft. Most can be made using materials you already have on hand. Chances are, though, that once you get started you'll find yourself collecting fabrics and flower components at craft stores, thrift shops, flea markets, hardware departments, garage sales… everywhere, in fact.

All the flowers in this book begin their life as either a long strip of fabric or as individual petals. Depending on the style, you'll cut fabric on the straight or the bias grain. Distinctive fabric flowers are created by folding, fringing, gathering, felting, edgestitching, or cutting strips and individual petals.

Your flowers can have centers or not, as you prefer. Ditto for the leaves. Most flowers in this book are assembled by stitching the pieces to a foundation— generally a stiff piece of fabric, such as buckram or heavyweight interfacing. Add a pin back or shoe clip if you like; or if you'd rather, stitch them directly onto a garment, and you're ready to move on to your next creation.

In this section, we'll take a general look at the materials you'll need to make fabric flowers. Most are things you already have in your sewing stash: fabrics, foundations, threads, notions, and findings. We'll also look at the equipment and supplies you'll need: cutting and measuring tools, pins, needles, a sewing machine (optional), and an iron. And finally, we'll look at some basic techniques: types of hand stitches, cutting techniques, edge finishes, types of centers, making different leaves, making bias tubes, and finishing your flowers.

In the Make a Flower! section that starts on page 22, we'll put these general techniques to use in creating specific flowers.

Materials

First, let's talk about the materials you'll need to start growing your own fabric flower garden.

● Fabrics

When it comes to choosing fabric, anything goes. You can make flowers from whatever captures your fancy. I've made flowers from scraps

left over

from a sewing project,

recycled clothing, and special

purchases intended just for

flowers. You don't have to prewash

the fabric or worry about whether it

will wrinkle. Most flowers can be made

with a minimum of fabric, just $\frac{1}{8}$ to $\frac{1}{4}$

yard. Flowers built up from individual

petals can generally be made entirely

from small scraps.

There are a number of considerations in choosing fabric for flowers. Color will probably be your primary concern. Check the color on both sides of the fabric; if the wrong side will show in the finished flower, choose a fabric that doesn't have an obvious back, unless you're deliberately seeking this effect.

Consider, too, whether the flower will look better made from shiny or dull fabric, and whether an opaque or sheer fabric works best.

Another consideration is the weight and thickness of the fabric. Thick or heavy fabrics will not gather tightly and thus may not be suitable for certain flower styles. The fabric's hand—how stiff or soft it is and how it drapes—also affects its suitability for a particular technique. Thin and soft fabrics without any body are perfect for some styles (for instance, the Flat Sparkling Flower on the opposite page and page 73), but not others. Sometimes a soft fabric can be starched or interfaced to add sufficient body. If you're in doubt about weight and hand, my advice is to make a sample.

The weave of a fabric is important for certain flowers, too. Weave refers to both the size of the criss-crossing threads that make up a fabric, as well as their density—in other words, how tightly they are woven. A very densely woven fabric will not gather well. A loosely woven fabric will ravel, which might be good or bad, depending on the effect you're after. For instance, Tweed (shown below and page 67) and Tweed Too (page 69) depend on loosely woven, thick threads to achieve their look.

Finally, the fiber content of your fabric could be important. If you're after sparkle, you may want a fabric woven from metallic fibers. If you want a felted flower, you'll need to start with wool. (To felt wool, wash it in hot water and dry in the dryer on high heat. This produces a thick

Here's a bouquet of felted flowers.

fabric that does not ravel.) Synthetic and novelty fabrics are available in a huge variety and are great fun for making flowers. A word of caution in using fabrics made from metallic and man-made fibers: they don't always press well. To be sure the fabric won't melt, first test a sample, using a low-heat setting on your iron.

● Foundations

Most of the time you'll stitch flowers to a small piece of backing to provide support; a backing also makes the flowers removable. Generally I use buckram, a heavily sized, loosely-woven fabric that is often available in the wedding section of fabric stores. I've also used heavy non-woven interfacing, as well as drapery-heading material (essentially a non-woven interfacing). Look for something that is non-raveling and stiff, but that can be sewn through by hand. For

most flowers you'll use a small piece (4 x 4 inches or less), and trim any excess during the finishing process.

● Threads

For hand sewing, I like to use good quality quilting thread (40 wt./3 ply) with a glazed finish. This type of thread is strong and does not easily tangle or knot during stitching. As a rule, match your thread color and fabric. If you can't find a match, use light-colored thread with light fabrics, and dark with dark; shades of grey often blend well.

When gathering by machine, I like to use the same type of quilting thread in the bobbin only. I generally use black bobbin thread for sewing dark colors and white or beige bobbin thread when sewing light-colored fabrics. For your top thread when gathering by machine, use a good quality sewing thread (50 wt./3 ply) that matches the color of the fabric. After stitching, pull on the bobbin thread to gather up the fabric; the quilting thread is stronger than the regular thread and thus less likely to break.

These petals are being sewn to a buckram backing.

Notions and Findings

This is a miscellaneous category that includes materials you can use to embellish and finish your flowers. For instance: buttons, beads, jewelry, pin backs, zipper tapes, stamens, yarns, ribbons—anything you want to use for flower centers and backs.

Equipment and Supplies

Let's move along to the tools of the trade. Here are a few items you'll need on hand to create those beauties.

Cutting and Measuring Tools

You'll need a good pair of sharp scissors to cut fabric, and a small pair of scissors or snips to cut threads. And you'll need a ruler and/or tape measure for measuring fabric strips and pieces.

A rotary-cutting set (cutter, mat, and ruler) is optional, but in my opinion this system is one of the greatest inventions since the sewing machine. These tools will speed up your cutting and make it more accurate; it's also easier on your hands than using scissors. The rotary cutter resembles a pizza cutter with a razor-sharp blade. The cutting mat is

Bias strips. Cut fabric at a 45° angle to the selvage. The bias grain of fabric is the least stable and will stretch, so take care handling your fabric when cutting. A rotary cutter greatly aids in accurately cutting on the bias. The natural stretch of bias-grain fabric is useful in many techniques, such as when making bias tubes. Also, bias-cut fabric does not ravel easily, eliminating the need to finish the edges.

● Edge Finishes

There are many ways to finish the edges of your flowers and leaves. The three methods I use in this book are raw, folded, and serged. For ease as well as efficiency, I cut strips the entire width of fabric (from selvage to selvage), finish the whole length of each strip in the technique of my choosing, and then cut to the lengths required for my project.

Raw. You can leave the edges raw or unfinished; this is a great effect for some projects. You may want to enhance the raw-edge effect by teasing out additional threads, making it more raggedy, even fringed. Fabrics woven from thick threads will have a more obvious ravel, or rough edge, than those woven from thin threads. Some fabrics (such as fleece, felt,

Fleece doesn't ravel and can be left unfinished.

A contrasting thread can be used to serge the raw edges of the fabric.

and boiled wool) do not fray or ravel, thus raw edges are an easy and obvious choice.

Another possibility for a raw-edge finish is to cut your strips and pieces on the bias grain. Bias edges do not ravel, though they may have a soft, subtle fray. Bias-cut strips will have a nice drape as well.

Folded. Edges can be finished with a fold. This can be accomplished either by folding a strip in half lengthwise and treating it as one layer, or by turning just the edge under and pressing. Note that this latter treatment (which I call a hem fold) does not involve stitching. Simply turn the edge under the amount desired and press well. Depending on the fabric, you may want to use spray starch to add body and to help hold down the pressed edge. Use this technique when the fabric is too thick to double or when you need to conserve fabric.

Serged. You can serge the edges of your fabric to finish them. This can be a very effective design element when you use decorative thread to blend or

A folded edge creates a crisp, polished flower.

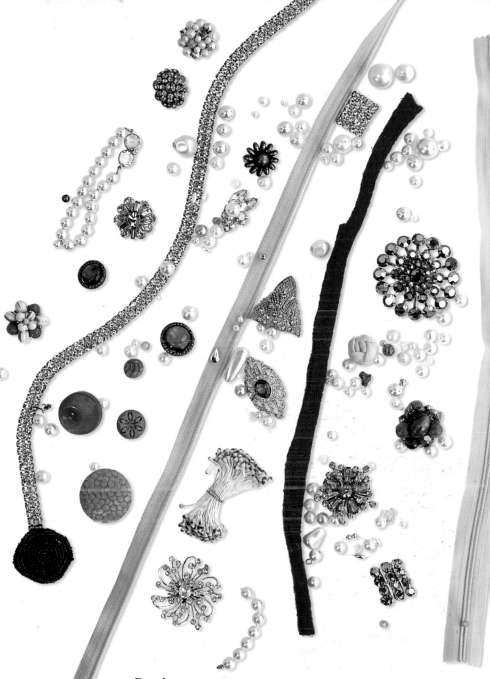

contrast with your fabric. Most often, I use a rolled-hem stitch on a single layer of fabric, but other serger stitches can be used as well.

• Centers

There are many things that can be used as a center for your flower. Some of the possibilities include:

Artificial stamens. These can be found in any craft or hobby store, in a variety of styles and colors.

Buttons. Use them as you find them, stack two or more to make colorful combinations, cover them with fabric (with or without padding), wrap them with decorative threads woven through the buttonholes, or glue sequins or jewels to them.

Beads. String them to make fanciful stamens, group them, or let large ones stand on their own.

Jewelry. Bits and pieces of random jewelry make unique centers. Check your own stash or shop flea markets and second-hand stores for earrings, brooches, and necklaces that can be taken apart.

Yarns and threads. Crochet chains to use as stamens, wind thick yarns into knots, or wrap decorative threads around beads and buttons.

Yo-yos. These small gathered circles of fabric are made using a traditional quilting technique, and can be used flat or stuffed. See the Sophisticated Yo-Yos for instructions (page 43).

Knotted fabric. Tie a short length of fabric into a knot; for larger knots, start with a longer piece, wrap the ends around the first knot, and tie again.

Ribbons and fabric strips. Use purchased ribbon, or tear fabric into narrow strips to create your own fuzzy-edged "ribbon." Pleat, scrunch, gather, and otherwise manipulate these ribbons to add texture to flower centers.

Zippers. Zippers? Yes! Cut a 20- to 22-inch nylon-coil zipper just above the zipper stop; unzip it to separate the zipper into two pieces (to make two centers). Begin rolling the tape tightly with the zipper teeth facing toward the outside. As you roll, use matching thread to securely stitch through the tape. When you get close to the end, fold the raw edge of the tape under; whipstitch to secure. To finish, stitch through the smooth (non-toothed) ends of the tape, pulling the edges in so they won't be seen from the top.

• Leaves

Fabric flowers can stand alone, or you can add leaves for additional color, texture, and realism. Following are instructions for five different styles; make a sixth by following the instructions for the Free-Motion Flower (page 25). Experiment with shapes, sizes, and fabrics to create even more variety. Edges can be left raw, folded, or serged (see Edge Finishes, page 14). Consider your fabric when deciding what type of leaf to make and how to finish the edges.

Basic leaf. This is the shape that probably comes to mind when you think about a leaf.

1. Cut a 6-inch square of fabric. Fold it in half, wrong sides together (figure 1). Press.

Figure 1

2. Fold the upper corners down to center bottom, forming a triangle with the folded edges meeting in the center (figure 2). Press. All raw edges are now along the bottom.

Figure 2

3. Stitch across the raw edge using a gathering stitch. Draw the fabric up tightly (figure 3). Tie off.

Figure 3

Hemmed-edge basic leaf variation. This leaf is ideal for thick fabrics that won't gather well if doubled (such as velvet). Cut the fabric into a 4 × 6-inch square. Press under 1 inch along one 6-inch side. Position it with the fold at the top, the hem facing up, and continue with steps 2 and 3, above.

Raw-edge basic leaf variation. Cut the fabric into a 3 × 6-inch square. Position the fabric wrong-side up, and continue with steps 2 and 3, above.

Wire-filled bias leaf. This leaf has an internal wire that allows bending and shaping.

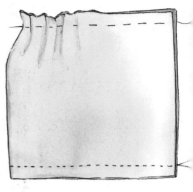

1. Cut a bias strip that is 4 × 8 inches. Fold it in half, right sides together, to create a 4-inch square. Stitch one side from the fold to the raw edge, using a ¼-inch seam allowance and a running stitch.

Figure 4

2. Hand stitch the opposite side of the fabric, from the fold to the raw edge, using a gathering stitch; pull up the fabric to gather, but do not tie off yet (figure 4). Turn the fabric pocket right-side out (figure 5).

3. Fold a 12-inch chenille stem in half; pinch the folded end to a sharp point Twist the loose ends together to create a short stem (approximately ½ inch). Bend out the sides to create a leaf shape (figure 6).

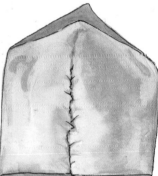

Figure 5

4. Slip the chenille stem inside the fabric pocket, positioning the point at the inside corner created by the first line of stitching (in step 1). Pull the fabric so both seams meet at the stem of the chenille stem, adjusting the gathers as necessary. Note that the fabric will seem too small for the chenille stem; stretch it to make it fit. (This is why the fabric *must be* cut on the bias.) Stitch through both seams to secure the fabric to the chenille stem. Tie off.

Figure 6

5. Stitch around the raw bottom edge one side at a time, using a gathering stitch (figure 7). Draw the fabric in tightly to the stem; tie off. Repeat for the other side (figure 8).

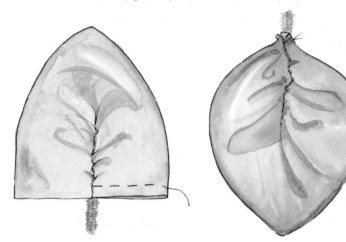

Figure 7   Figure 8

Old-fashioned leaf. This is a rounded, ruffled-looking leaf, reminiscent of a Victorian garden.

1. Cut a strip that's 3 x 14 inches. Fold it in half lengthwise, wrong sides together; press. Fold it in half widthwise (figure 9); press. The strip is now 1½ x 7 inches and four layers thick.

Figure 9

2. Stitch the short side close to the raw edge using a running stitch, through all layers; tie off securely, but do not cut the thread. Continue stitching the long raw edge toward the fold using a gathering stitch (figure 10).

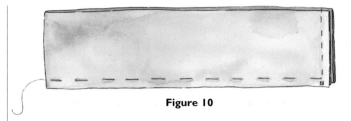

Figure 10

3. Draw the fabric up tightly along the long edge. Tie off. Pull the leaf open at the folded edges (figure 11). Press if necessary.

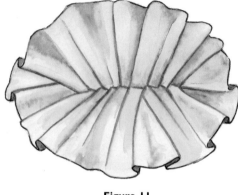

Figure 11

Pointed leaf. This one is similar to the old-fashioned leaf, but with two pointed ends.

1. Cut a strip that is 3 x 14 inches. Fold it in half lengthwise, wrong sides together; press. Fold it in half widthwise; press. The strip is now 1½ x 7 inches and four layers thick.

2. Fold the narrow ends up to meet the folded edge (creating a 45° angle); pin if desired. Press. The strip now looks like a little boat (figure 12).

Figure 12

3. Starting at the upper right, stitch one short side close to the folded edge using a running stitch, through all layers; tie off securely, but do not cut the thread. Continue stitching along the raw edge using a gathering stitch. Pull to gather the fabric along the raw edge tightly; tie off but do not cut the thread. Continue stitching along the remaining short side, close to the folded edge using a running stitch, through all layers; tie off (figure 13).

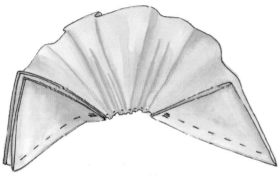

Figure 13

4. Trim off the excess fabric—the small triangles—close to the running-stitch lines on both short ends. Pull the leaf open at the folded edges (figure 14). Press if necessary.

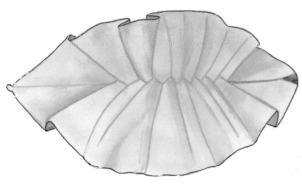

Figure 14

Five-petal leaf. This leaf forms a delightful ruff around fabric flowers.

Refer to instructions for the Wonderful Wool Flower (page 47). This is a good example of how leaf and flower patterns can be interchanged by using different colors and fabrics.

● **Bias Tubes**

Bias tubes are fun both for making and embellishing fabric flowers. Make them thick or thin, fill them with cording or leave them empty, and vary colors to add interest to your creations. Empty, they add texture when looped and stitched behind a flower, such as the Striped and Gathered Flower (page 31). Corded, they can be used to create flowers such as the Loopy Flower (page 87). To make bias tubes:

1. Cut the fabric on the bias, 2 inches wide by the desired length. Fold it in half lengthwise, right sides together. Stitch with a sewing machine, using the folded edge of fabric as your guide. In other words, align the fold with the edge of your presser foot, a marking on your throat plate, or whatever gives you the width of tubing that you want. Stretch the bias strip as you sew, to prevent the stitches from breaking when you turn the tube right side out.

2. Turn the tube right side out using whatever method you prefer. I like to use a big-eyed needle and heavy thread. I whipstitch one end of the bias tube, and then slip the eye (rather than the sharp point) of the needle inside the tube through the whipstitched end, pushing the needle down through the tube until it emerges at the other end. Then I simply pull the thread, sliding the fabric back on itself until the tube is right-side out. Roll the tube between the palms of your hands to smooth it out.

Corded bias tubes. In this method, you begin near the middle of a long piece of cording, so you need twice as much cording as you'll actually cover. Once the tube is stitched, you'll slide the fabric backward over the uncovered cording. So, if you're purchasing cording for a specific project, you'll need a piece that's twice as long as your desired finished length, plus about 6 inches. As a rule, consider 36 inches the maximum finished length for covered cording; longer lengths are difficult to turn. It sounds complicated, but it's not! It's easier to do than explain.

1. Cut the width of the bias strip at least 1½ inches larger than the circumference of your cording, by the desired length.

2. From one end of the cording, measure off the desired length plus 3 inches; mark this spot with a fabric pen or a straight pin as indicated in figure 15. Do not cut the cording.

3. Just past the marked spot, begin wrapping the bias strip around the cording, right sides together. Using a sewing machine and a zipper foot, stitch across the end of the bias strip nearest the pin, sewing through all layers (including the cording). Pivot when you get about ¼ inch from the long edge of the fabric; angle your line of stitching back toward the cording (this triangle at the beginning gives the fabric a place to go when you're turning the tube later). Continue stitching the entire length of the bias strip, staying close to the cording and stretching the fabric as you sew (figure 15). Trim the raw edges if necessary.

Figure 15

4. Remove the pin. Turn by pulling on the cording, sliding the fabric back over the beginning portion of your cording (figure 16). Cut off the excess cording.

Figure 16

● Finishing

Most flowers will be finished by stitching the elements onto a foundation (see Foundations, page 10) using a stab stitch and matching thread. Start by stitching down the background pieces, such as the leaves. Then attach the flower, and finally the center. When all the pieces are attached, trim the foundation to the desired size.

There's no need to overdo your stitching when securing elements to the foundation. Remember, nobody's going to be playing tug-o-war with your flowers!

To make flowers removable, I often add a pin backing. Here's how:

1. Trim the foundation into a round or oval shape.

2. Cut a square of felt or faux suede a bit larger than the trimmed foundation.

3. Cut two small slits in the felt or faux suede, where you want the pin to be. Thread the pin back down

Figure 17

through one slit and up through the other, so the back is behind the felt/faux suede and the pin is on right side. Glue the pin back to the wrong side of the material (figure 17).

4. Glue the wrong side of the felt or faux suede to the foundation. When dry, trim the excess a bit larger than the foundation (figure 18).

Figure 18

● Craft a Flower

Now that you know the basics, you're ready to create your own flowers. The Make a Flower! section contains detailed instructions for making 36 different flowers, grouped into 13 general types: Free-Motion, Gathered, Yo-Yo, Five-Petal, Roses, Ruched, Individual-Petal, Pansies, Folded-Petal, Loopy, Bias-Strip, Poppy, and Felt Flowers. The first set of instructions for each type of flower usually has the general directions to make the other projects in its category. For example, in the Five-Petal category, the Wonderful Wool Flower has the basic construction directions for the four variations that follow. You'll be referred back to the proper set of instructions as needed. To entice you, a preview of the flower types is on the next page.

I'm sure you'll recognize some garden favorites among these flowers, and others are products of pure imagination. Once you're comfortable with the techniques, feel free to improvise, change dimensions, add leaves and other embellishments, and mix-and-match elements to create your own one-of-a-kind floral fantasies.

Make a Flower!

Use the flower projects on the following pages to spark your imagination. They are divided into 13 categories:

Free-Motion Flower. This flower is created by "drawing" with your sewing machine.

Gathered Flowers. The eight flowers in this category are based on a simple gathering technique.

Yo-Yo Flowers. Two projects explore the use of the yo-yo, which is a traditional form used by quilters.

Five-Petal Flowers. A creative pattern of gathering stitches results in a lovely bloom. Five distinct variations show the versatility of this technique.

Roses. No book on fabric flowers would be complete without the classic rose form, shown here in two variations.

Ruched Flowers. Another pattern of gathering stitches allows you to make two different blooms.

Individual-Petal Flowers. You can really get creative when you build flowers one petal at a time, as you see in the six projects in this category.

Pansies. This garden favorite in rendered two ways, the classic pansy form and a contemporary version.

Folded-Petal Flowers. Three different folding techniques give you three very different flowers.

Loopy Flower. Just for fun, make a cheerful flower from bias-covered cording.

Bias-Strip Flowers. Use strips cut from the bias to create two chic modern flowers.

Poppy. Learn to make this springtime beauty and create your own bouquet.

Felt Flower. The simple graphic shapes that form this flower can be used in any color scheme.

free-motion flower

A layer of sheer fabric adds sparkle and depth to flowers you draw using your sewing machine. This technique is called *free-motion embroidery*.

what you need

- Sewing machine with a darning foot
- Fabric and thread, for practice
- 2 fabrics, 1 a base and 1 a sheer overlay, cut a bit larger than your hoop
- Spring-tension embroidery hoop, several inches larger than your flower
- Chalk
- Contrasting thread
- Scissors

what you do

1. To practice free-motion embroidery, first lower (or cover, depending on your sewing machine) the feed dogs. With the feed dogs disengaged, the sewing machine will not be pulling the fabric under the needle; rather, your hands move the fabric in whatever direction you want. To get the feel of it, practice moving your fabric with a slow and steady motion while running the machine fairly fast.

2. Try writing your name in script; we know how to write our names almost instinctively. Practice creating even stitches. Next, try circles and other shapes. Try going over your previous stitching to get a solid line. Now, try filling in a shape. Practice until you're comfortable drawing the shapes you want by moving the fabric under the needle.

3. To create a flower, lay the sheer fabric on top of the base fabric, right sides up. Place them together in the hoop with the spring-side up, so that the fabric is flat against the bed of the sewing machine.

4. Draw the desired flower shape onto the fabric with chalk (figure 1).

5. Free-motion stitch around each petal shape about five times. If desired, change the thread color and stitch the center of the flower and the veins on the petals.

6. Remove the stitched fabric from the hoop (figure 2). Trim the flower about ⅛ inch outside of your stitching.

tip
Use this same technique to make leaves.

Figure 1

Figure 2

dreamy dupioni

Easy and versatile, this gathering technique can be used to make everything from a classic Cabbage Rose to its fuzzy, contemporary cousin on the next page.

what you need

- Scissors
- 2 x 36-inch strip of bias-cut silk dupioni fabric
- Sewing machine or needle and thread
- Approximately 4-inch square of foundation fabric
- Pin back (optional)

what you do

1. Trim the ends of your fabric to a gentle curve. Stitch along the curved edge using a gathering stitch, as shown in figure 1.

2. Gather the fabric tightly. Roll the gathered edge around on itself (figure 2), stitching to secure it as you go.

3. Stitch the flower to the foundation. Shape it with additional hand stitches as desired. Trim any excess foundation fabric.

4. Add a pin back if desired.

Figure 2

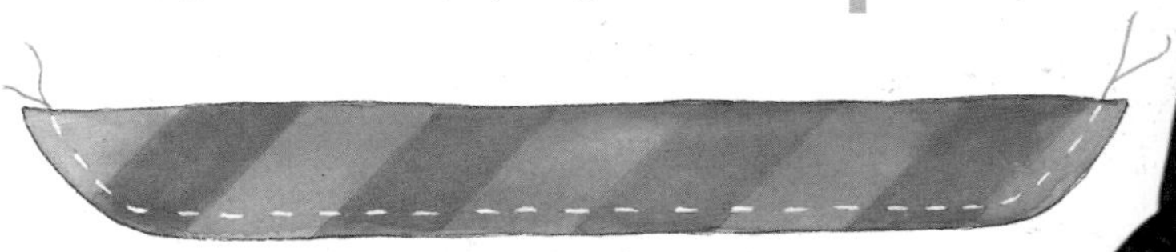

Figure 1

fuzzy cuties

fuzzy and felted

Put an old wool sweater to new use by cutting off the waistband and felting it, creating an unusual fabric for these fuzzy cuties.

what you need

- Waistband of a wool sweater, approximately 2 x 36 inches
- Sewing machine or needle and thread
- Scissors
- Approximately 4-inch square of foundation fabric
- Sparkly bead or button
- Pin back (optional)

what you do

1. Felt the wool waistband by washing it in hot water and then drying it on high heat.

2. Follow the instructions for the Dreamy Dupioni Flower (page 27), steps 1 through 3.

3. Stitch a sparkly bead or button at the center, through all layers.

4. Add a pin back if desired.

striped and gathered

Stripes are striking when set off by a neutral edge. This flower is further enhanced with bias tubes that are looped to create fanciful leaves.

what you need

- Sewing machine or needle and thread
- 7 bias tubes for leaves, 3 of striped fabric and 4 of solid, each approximately ¼ x 9 inches when finished
- 2½ x 36-inch strip of striped fabric
- 3½ x 36-inch strip of solid fabric
- Iron
- Approximately 4-inch square of foundation fabric
- Scissors
- Pin back (optional)

what you do

1. Make the bias tubes following the instructions on page 19.

2. Stitch the two fabric strips right sides together along one long edge using a ½-inch seam allowance. Press the seam allowances toward the solid fabric. Fold the solid fabric over the seam allowance (fabrics will be wrong sides together); press. Trim the raw edges if necessary.

3. Follow the instructions for the Dreamy Dupioni Flower (page 27), steps 1 and 2, treating the two layers of fabric as one.

4. Bring the ends of each bias tube together; whipstitch to secure. Stitch these loops to the foundation. Stitch the flower over the loops. Trim any excess foundation fabric.

5. Add a pin back if desired.

totally tonal

Use two tones of the same color fabric to create a flower with subtle elegance. Include a couple of leaves in the same color for additional fullness.

what you need

- Dark fabric, 2 pieces that are 2 x 6½ inches each (to make 2 bias tubes for leaves); 2 pieces that are 6 x 6 inches each (for leaves); and 1 piece that is a 2½ x 36-inch strip (for flower)

- Light fabric, 2 pieces that are 2 x 6½ inches each (to make 2 bias tubes for leaves) and 1 piece that is a 3 x 36-inch strip (for flower)

- Sewing machine or needle and thread

- Iron

- Approximately 4-inch square of foundation fabric

- Scissors

- Pin back (optional)

what you do

1. Make the bias tubes following the instructions on page 19.

2. Make two basic leaves following the instructions on page 16.

3. Stitch the two fabric strips right sides together along one long edge using a ¼-inch seam allowance. Press the seam allowances toward the lighter fabric. Fold the lighter fabric over the seam allowance (fabrics will be wrong sides together); press. Trim the raw edges if necessary.

4. Follow the instructions for the Dreamy Dupioni Flower (page 27), steps 1 and 2, treating the two layers of fabric as one.

5. Bring the ends of each bias tube together; whipstitch to secure. Stitch these loops to the foundation. Stitch the leaves to the foundation, offset from the loops. Stitch the flower over the leaves and loops. Trim any excess foundation fabric.

6. Add a pin back if desired.

folded-edge flower

The fold of this fabric gives a neat and clean edge to this business-like, yet still soft, flower.

what you need

- Sewing machine or needle and thread
- 4 x 36 inch strip of fabric for flower
- 2 rectangles of bias-cut fabric for leaves, each 4 x 8 inches
- Iron
- Approximately 4-inch square of foundation fabric
- 3 strings of seed beads for center, each approximately 2 inches long
- Scissors
- Pin back (optional)

what you do

1. Make two wire-filled bias leaves following the instructions on page 17.

2. Fold the fabric in half lengthwise; press. Follow the instructions for the Dreamy Dupioni Flower (page 27), steps 1 and 2, treating the two layers of fabric as one.

3. Stitch the leaves to the foundation; stitch the flower to the foundation over the leaves. Stitch the three strings of beads to the center. Trim any excess foundation fabric.

4. Add a pin back if desired.

softness

camellia

These pastel beauties evoke fragrant camellias. The raw-edge finish adds softness that enhances the effect.

what you need

- Sewing machine or needle and thread
- 2 x 36-inch bias-cut strip of fabric for flower
- 2 rectangles of bias-cut fabric for leaves, each 3 x 6 inches
- 2 x 8 inch strip of fabric for center
- Iron
- Scissors
- Approximately 1-inch square of foundation fabric
- Pin back (optional)

what you do

1. Make two raw-edge basic leaves, following the instructions on page 17.

2. Follow the instructions for the Dreamy Dupioni Flower (page 27), steps 1 and 2.

3. Make the fabric center by folding in the long raw edges of the fabric strip so they meet in the middle. (See figure 1 on page 57 for an illustration of this technique.) Twist this folded strip loosely; tie one or more knots to make a center the size desired and trim any excess fabric. Shape the knot with small stitches in matching thread if desired.

4. Stitch the leaves to the foundation; stitch the flower to the foundation over the leaves; and stitch the center, cut ends down, to the flower through all layers. Trim any excess foundation fabric.

5. Add a pin back if desired.

watercolor

watercolor flower

For added fullness and depth, use two strips in related shades to make up a single flower.

what you need

- Sewing machine or needle and thread
- 2 × 12-inch bias-cut strip of dark fabric for inner flower
- 2 × 36-inch bias-cut strip of light fabric for outer flower
- 2 rectangles of fabric for leaves, each 2 × 10 inches
- Approximately 4-inch square of foundation fabric
- Scissors
- Pin back (optional)

what you do

1. Make two raw-edge old-fashioned leaves following the instructions on page 18, with the following change to step 1: Cut a strip that's 2 × 10 inches and fold in half so the strip is 2 × 5 inches. Continue as directed in steps 2 and 3.

2. Follow the instructions for the Dreamy Dupioni Flower (page 27), step 1, for both the inner-flower and the outer-flower strips. Complete step 2 for the inner-flower strip. Gather the outer-flower strip and roll and stitch the gathered edge around the inner strip.

3. Stitch the leaves to the foundation; stitch the flower to the foundation over the leaves. Trim any excess foundation fabric.

4. Add a pin back if desired.

dainty velvet blossom

Change the size of your gathered flowers by changing the dimensions of your fabric strip. ❧

what you need

- Sewing machine or needle and thread
- 2 rectangles of fabric for leaves, each 3 x 6 inches
- Iron
- 4 x 22-inch strip of velvet for flower
- Approximately 4-inch square of foundation fabric
- Scissors
- Pin back (optional)

what you do

1. Make two raw-edge basic leaves following the instructions on page 17.

2. Fold the fabric in half lengthwise; press. Follow the instructions for the Dreamy Dupioni Flower (page 27), steps 1 and 2, treating the two layers of fabric as one.

3. Stitch the leaves to the foundation; stitch the flower to the foundation over the leaves. Trim any excess foundation fabric.

4. Add a pin back if desired.

sophisticated yo-yos

Yo-yos are very versatile, equally at home starring as flowers or playing a supporting role as centers. Group them in clusters for added impact.

what you need

- Scissors

- 3 circles of fabric for flowers, each approximately 3½ inches in diameter (finished yo-yo is approximately half the size of the starting circle)

- Needle and thread

- 2 squares of metallic fabric for leaves, each 6 x 6 inches

- Approximately 3-inch square of foundation fabric

- 3 medium-sized pearls

- Pin back (optional)

what you do

1. Cut the fabric circles (figure 1). For each, turn under a scant ¼ inch at the edge of each circle, wrong sides together. Stitch around the folded edge using a gathering stitch. The longer the stitch, the tighter the circle will gather. Gather the fabric tightly; tie off. Flatten the yo-yo, centering the hole on top (figure 2).

2. Make two basic leaves following the instructions on page 16.

3. Stitch the leaves to the foundation. Stitch the three Yo-Yo Flowers on top of the leaves and stitch a pearl at the center of each flower, through all layers. Trim any excess foundation fabric.

4. Add a pin back if desired.

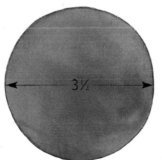

Figure 1

Figure 2

pouffy pods

You'd hardly recognize these charming buds as yo-yos. They've been transformed by finishing them upside-down, adding stuffing, and embellishing with thick thread.

what you need

- Serger, with rolled-edge stitch
- Needle and thread
- 3 circles of fabric for flowers, each approximately 2¼ inches in diameter
- Stuffing for center
- 2 x 25½-inch strip of fabric for leaves
- Approximately 3-inch square of foundation fabric
- Thick decorative thread, such as embroidery floss
- 9 small beads
- Scissors
- Pin back (optional)

what you do

1. Finish one long edge of the leaf fabric with your serger, using a rolled-edge stitch. Make a five-petal leaf following instructions for the Wonderful Wool Flower, steps 1 and 2, page 47, positioning the serged edge where the fold is in figure 1.

2. For each fabric circle, stitch around the raw edges using a gathering stitch; the longer the stitch, the tighter the circle will gather. Place a small bit of stuffing in the center and draw the fabric up around it. Add more or less stuffing as desired; gather the fabric tightly and tie off. The gathered edge is the bottom of the flower.

3. Stitch the leaves to the foundation. Use thick, decorative thread to stitch the three pods on top of the leaves as follows: Stitch from underneath the foundation up through the center of the pod; insert the needle back through the foundation close to the first stitch, wrapping the thread around the pod in the process. Do this a total of five times, wrapping the pod in different spots to create a star design with the thread. Finish by stitching three beads at the center of each flower, through all layers. Trim any excess foundation fabric.

4. Add a pin back if desired.

> **tip**
>
> As seen below, substitute four small basic leaves (page 16, using a 3-inch rather than a 6-inch square) for the five-petal leaf in step 1 to change the look of your Pouffy Pod.

classic posy

wonderful wool flower

This is a classic posy that takes on a whole range of looks depending on fabrics, finishes, and embellishments. Wool might seem an unlikely fabric choice for a flower, but it gathers beautifully.

what you need

- 4 x 25½-inch strip of wool houndstooth check
- Iron
- Pins
- Needle and thread
- Approximately 4-inch square of foundation fabric
- Approximately ½ x 12-inch strip of thick, felted wool for center
- Scissors
- Pin back (optional)

what you do

1. Press the houndstooth check in half lengthwise. Starting ¼ inch in from the cut edge, mark with a pin every 5 inches. Stitch around the pins using a gathering stitch. Remove the pins (figure 1).

2. Draw the fabric up tightly to form a circle with five petal shapes (figure 2). Note that the thicker your fabric is, the harder it will be to gather tightly, you can adjust the size of your center to cover the space in the middle.

3. Stitch the flower to the foundation fabric.

4. Coil the felted-wool strip to create a center; stitch it to the middle of the flower, through all layers. Trim any excess foundation fabric.

5. Add a pin back if desired.

Figure 1

Figure 2

funky fabric

48

flower gone wild

Take your flower for a walk on the wild side by choosing a funky printed fabric.

what you need

- Needle and thread
- 4 x 25½-inch strip of print fabric
- Approximately 1-inch square of foundation fabric
- Circle of fabric for center; 3½ inches in diameter
- Scissors
- Pin back (optional)

what you do

1. Follow the instructions for the Wonderful Wool Flower, steps 1 through 3 (page 47).

2. Make a yo-yo (page 43, step 1) for the center; stitch it to the middle of the flower, through all layers. Trim any excess foundation fabric.

3. Add a pin back if desired.

luxurious

victorian vision

Use luxurious fabric and vintage lace for a romantic interpretation of this technique.

what you need

- Needle and thread
- Doily
- Approximately 4-inch square of foundation fabric
- 2 squares of metallic fabric for leaves, each 6 x 6 inches
- 4 x 25½-inch strip of velvet
- Iron
- 2 circles of fabric for center, each 3½ inches in diameter, 1 of velvet and 1 of sheer metallic
- Stuffing for center
- Scissors
- Pin back (optional)

what you do

1. Stitch the doily to the foundation fabric.

2. Make two basic leaves (page 16). Stitch them in place on top of the doily, through the foundation fabric.

3. Make the flower from your velvet strip, following the instructions for the Wonderful Wool Flower, steps 1 through 3 (page 47). Stitch the flower to the foundation, on top of the doily and leaves, through all layers.

4. Make a stuffed yo-yo center (page 45, step 2), first placing the sheer fabric on top of the velvet to create a moiré effect. Stitch it to the middle of the flower, through all layers. Trim any excess foundation fabric.

5. Add a pin back if desired.

perfectly petite

Make different-sized flowers by varying the dimensions of your starting strip. This petite beauty features a sparkling yo-yo center.

what you need

- Needle and thread
- Iron
- 3 x 20½-inch strip of metallic mesh fabric
- Approximately 4-inch square of foundation fabric
- Circle of fabric for center, 3½ inches in diameter
- ¾-inch button with 4 holes
- Decorative thread
- Scissors
- Pin back or shoe clip (optional)

what you do

1. Follow the instructions for the Wonderful Wool Flower, steps 1 through 3 (page 47), except place your marks 4 inches apart in step 1.

2. Make a yo-yo (page 43, step 1) for the center; slip the button inside the yo-yo before drawing up the gathering thread, then tie off. Stitch the button-filled yo-yo to the middle of the flower, through all layers, using a decorative thread in a criss-cross pattern through the button's holes. Trim any excess foundation fabric.

3. Add a pin back or shoe clip if desired.

ragged edges

frayed flower

The ragged edges of this flower can be subtle or pronounced depending on how much your fabric ravels.

what you need

- Needle and thread
- 2 x 25 ½-inch strip of bias-cut fabric
- Approximately 1-inch square of foundation fabric
- 1½ x 10-inch strip of soft netting for center
- ⅜-inch button
- Scissors
- Pin back (optional)

what you do

1. Follow the instructions for the Wonderful Wool Flower, steps 1 through 3 (page 47); as this flower is made from only one layer of fabric, ignore the press-in-half direction in step 1.

2. Fold the netting strip in half lengthwise. Stitch along the fold using a gathering stitch; draw the fabric up tightly and tie off. Shape it into a circle and stitch it to the center of the flower, through all layers.

3. Sew the button to the center, through all layers. Trim any excess foundation fabric.

4. Add a pin back if desired.

grey folded rose

This folding technique—as clever as it is fun—creates a lovely rose blossom.

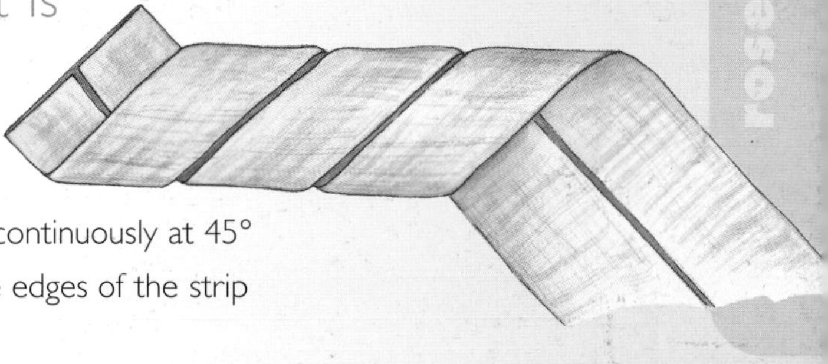

what you need

- Sewing machine or needle and thread
- 4 x 45-inch strip of fabric
- Iron
- 2 squares of fabric for leaves, each 6 x 6 inches
- Approximately 4-inch square of foundation fabric
- Artificial stamens for center
- Scissors
- Pin back (optional)

what you do

1. Make two basic leaves following the instructions on page 16.

2. Fold in both long edges of the flower fabric so they meet at the center of the strip (figure 1); press.

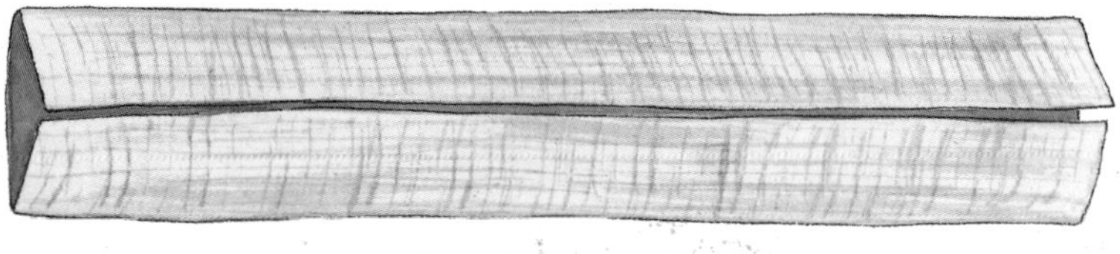

3. Fold the strip continuously at 45° angles around the edges of the strip (figure 2).

4. Stitch one short and one long side using a gathering stitch (figure 3).

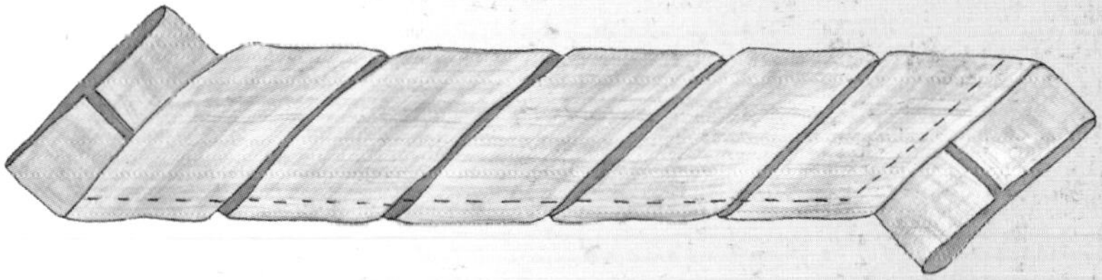

Figure 2

5. Gather the fabric tightly; tie off. Roll the gathered edge around on itself, stitching to secure the roll as you go.

6. Stitch the leaves to the foundation. Stitch the flower on top of the leaves, and then the stamens to the center, through all layers. Trim any excess foundation fabric.

7. Add a pin back if desired.

Figure 3

Figure 1

classic rose

Double the fullness of a folded rose by adding a second strip of fabric. It's shown here in a classic rose-colored fabric.

what you need

- Sewing machine or needle and thread
- 2 strips of fabric, each 4 x 45 inches
- Iron
- Approximately 4-inch square of foundation fabric
- Scissors
- Pin back (optional)

what you do

1. Follow the instructions for the Grey Folded Rose, steps 2 through 4, page 57, for both fabric strips.

2. Gather the fabric tightly in each strip; tie off. Starting with one of the strips, roll the gathered edge around on itself, stitching to secure the roll as you go. Roll and stitch the second strip around the first.

3. Stitch the flower to the foundation. Trim any excess foundation fabric.

4. Add a pin back if desired.

Variation

Created in white, these roses are the perfect adornment for a wedding gown.

peony

Revive the old-fashioned technique of ruching to make these beautifully full flowers. Think peonies in the spring.

what you need

- Sewing machine or needle and thread
- 3 x 45-inch strip of fabric, torn rather than cut
- Approximately 4-inch square of foundation fabric
- Bead(s) for center
- Scissors
- Pin back or shoe clip (optional)

what you do

1. Use a gathering stitch to sew from one edge of the fabric to the other at a 45° angle (figure 1); continue for the length of the strip.

2. Gather the fabric tightly to form petals; tie off.

3. Roll the gathered edge around on itself, pushing the petals to face up as necessary, and stitching to secure the roll as you go.

4. Stitch the flower to the foundation. Stitch one large or several small beads to the center, through all layers. Trim any excess foundation fabric.

5. Add a pin back or shoe clip if desired.

tip

Make these flowers larger or smaller by increasing or decreasing the dimensions of the starting strip.

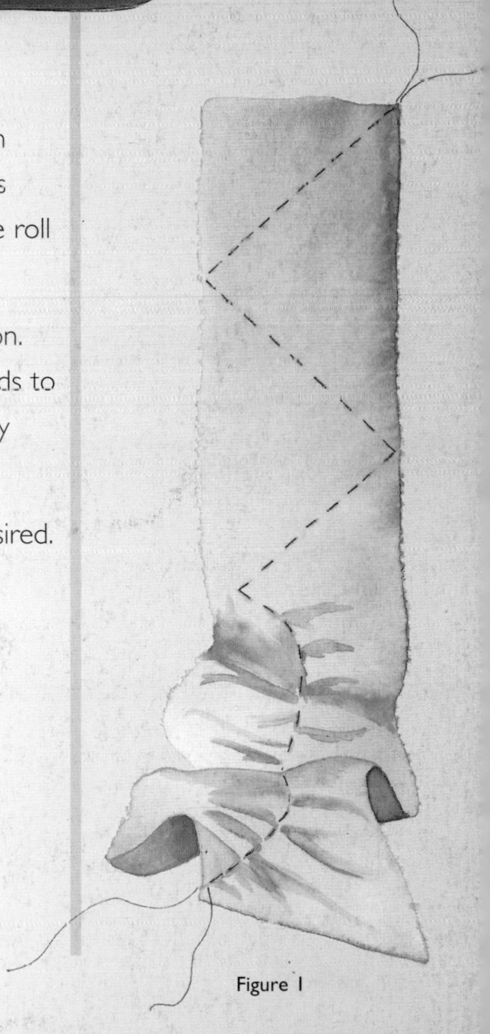

Figure 1

polka dot peony

Use your serger to add a decorative-thread finish to the petals on this flower.

what you need

- Sewing machine or needle and thread
- Serger, set up for a rolled edge stitch
- Decorative thread
- 3 x 15-inch strip of fabric
- Approximately 4-inch square of foundation fabric
- Scissors
- Pin back (optional)

what you do

1. Stitch both long edges of your fabric strip using the serger and a rolled-edge stitch.

2. Follow the instructions for the Peony, steps 1 through 5, page 61, eliminating the beaded center in step 4.

tip

Experiment with other serger stitches and a variety of threads to finish your flower edges.

fun fleece flower

Build these up petal by petal for as delicate or frilly a flower as you like. In this variation, thick fleece or felted fabric produces a flower so substantial it doesn't need a foundation.

what you need

- Scissors
- Approximately ⅛ yard of thick, non-raveling fabric (such as felted wool or fleece)
- Needle and thread
- Button or stamens for center (optional)
- Pin back (optional)

what you do

1. Cut the individual petals using the pattern in figure 1 as a guide. You'll need approximately 15 petals for each flower, depending on the size or fullness you wish. If you want, graduate the size of petals—from smaller at the center to fuller on the outside.

2. Beginning with the inside petal, stitch along the bottom edge using a gathering stitch. When you're approximately halfway across, overlap the next petal and continue stitching through both layers. Repeat this process (figure 2) until you have all of your petals strung on the gathering thread. Draw the fabric up tightly and tie off.

3. Roll the gathered edge around on itself from inside to outside, shaping the petals and stitching to secure the roll as you go.

4. Stitch a button or stamens at the center, if desired.

5. Add a pin back if desired.

Figure 1
Enlarge 200%

Figure 2

tip

This technique can produce a wide variety of looks depending on the fabric, the shape and number of petals, and your center. The next five projects demonstrate the versatility of this method.

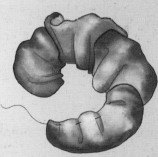

loosely woven

tweed

The raw edges of a loosely woven silk-tweed fabric fray easily, giving this version of the Individual-Petal Flower an entirely different look. Add a surprise by featuring the seam allowance, rather than the finished edge, of commercial piping for your center.

what you need

- Scissors
- Approximately ⅛ yard of silk tweed fabric
- Needle and thread
- Approximately 4-inch square of foundation fabric
- Approximately 8 to 12 inches of ⅛-inch satin piping for center ruff
- Approximately ⅜-inch bead or button for center
- Pin back (optional)

what you do

1. Follow the instructions for the Fun Fleece Flower steps 1 through 3, page 65, overlapping the petals by ¼ inch in step 2.

2. Stitch the flower to the foundation.

3. Gather the piping by drawing the fabric up tightly along the cord; knot the cord to secure. Trim off the excess cording and hide the ends in the fabric. Stitch this ruff to the center of the flower, through all layers.

4. Stitch a button to the center of the ruff, through all layers.

5. Add a pin back if desired.

tip

For a custom color-match, make your own piping for the center. Cut a bias strip 2 x 8-to-12 inches and fold it in half lengthwise, wrong sides together. Stitch rat-tail cord snugly into the fold using a zipper foot.

tweed too

Centers are fun to play with, and can completely change the look of your flowers.

what you need

- Scissors
- Approximately ⅛ yard of silk tweed fabric
- Needle and thread
- Approximately 4-inch square of foundation fabric
- Approximately ½ x 12 inches of sheer fabric for center ruff, torn on both long edges
- 3 buttons for center, approximately ¼ to ⅜ inches each
- Pin back (optional)

what you do

1. Follow the instructions for Fun Fleece Flower, steps 1 through 3, page 65, overlapping the petals by ¼ inch in step 2.

2. Stitch the flower to the foundation.

3. Stitch the torn fabric strip to the center of the flower, through all layers, looping it randomly around the center to create a ruff.

4. Stitch the three buttons to the center of the ruff, through all layers.

5. Add a pin back if desired.

crinkly metallic

marvelous metallic

Use a crinkly, metallic fabric for a techno-looking flower.

what you need

- Scissors
- Approximately ⅛ yard of crinkly, metallic fabric
- Needle and thread
- Approximately 4-inch square of foundation fabric
- Button for center
- Pin back (optional)

what you do

1. Cut the individual petals using the pattern on page 65 as a guide. You'll need approximately 11 petals, depending on your fabric.

2. Stitch the petals together along the bottom edge using a gathering stitch, one after another, until you have all the petals strung on the gathering thread. Draw the fabric up tightly, creating a flat circle of petals, and tie off.

3. Stitch the flower to the foundation. Stitch the button to the center of the flower, through all layers.

4. Add a pin back if desired.

charmeuse

flat sparkling flower

Soft silk charmeuse shines in this adaptation of the Individual-Petal Flower. Play with the shape of your petals to liven things up, too.

what you need

- Scissors
- Approximately ⅛ yard of silk charmeuse fabric
- Needle and thread
- Approximately 4-inch square of foundation fabric
- Rhinestone button for center
- Pin back (optional)

what you do

1. Cut the individual petals using the pattern as a guide (figure 1). You'll need approximately 5 petals, depending on your fabric.

2. Follow the instructions for the Marvelous Metallic Flower, steps 2 through 4, page 71.

Figure I
Enlarge 200%

full silky flower

A sparkly rhinestone button is a perfect foil for this luxuriously full silk charmeuse flower. This is a great use for those mail-order fabric samples.

what you need

- Scissors
- Approximately ¼ yard of silk charmeuse fabric
- Needle and thread
- Approximately 4-inch square of foundation fabric
- Rhinestone button for center
- Pin back (optional)

what you do

1. Follow the instructions for the Flat Sparkling Flower, steps 1 and 2, but substitute approximately two dozen petals for the five specified in step 1. Scallop the edges of the petals as desired.

traditional pansy

Who can resist smiling back at a pansy? Add a few of these sunny faces to a hat or lapel to brighten everyone's day.

what you need

- Iron
- 5 strips of fabric, each 2 x 4 inches, 3 of purple and 2 of lavender
- Scissors
- Needle and thread
- Approximately 3-inch square of foundation fabric
- 6 inches of ¼- or ⅛-inch-wide yellow ribbon for center
- Pin back or shoe clip (optional)

what you do

1. Press the strips in half lengthwise, wrong sides together. Cut both ends of each piece at a 45° angle, cutting in from the folded edge.

2. Position two purple strips with their folded edges to the inside, their corner edges matching, to create a V shape. Stitch close to the raw edges using a gathering stitch, around the entire V, beginning at a folded edge (figure 1).

3. Gather the fabric tightly; tie off. Shape the petals using your fingers. Stitch them to the foundation (figure 2).

4. Lay the lavender strips vertically on the table, with their folded edges facing each other. Lay the remaining purple strip over them at the top, with the folded edge facing down. Reposition the strips so that the raw corner edges match, creating an upside-down U shape. Stitch close to the raw edges using a gathering stitch, around the entire U, beginning at the folded edge of one of the lavender strips (figure 3).

5. Gather the fabric tightly; tie off. Shape the petals using your fingers (figure 4). Stitch the petals to the foundation on top of those from step 3.

6. Overlap the ends of the ribbon by about ½ inch, forming a circle. Using matching thread, stitch the ends together; continue stitching along the length of the ribbon, at center, using a gathering stitch. Draw the ribbon up tightly. Stitch the gathered ribbon to the center of the flower, through all layers. Trim any excess foundation fabric.

7. Add a pin back or shoe clip if desired.

variation

Reverse the color scheme if you want, as you see on the shoe at the right.

Figure 1

Figure 2

Figure 3

Figure 4

silk shantung

raw-edge pansy

Shiny silk shantung is the perfect fabric for making pansies with a soft, raw-edge finish.

what you need

- Needle and thread
- 5 strips of bias-cut fabric, each 1½ x 6 inches, 3 in one color and 2 in another color
- Scissors
- Approximately 3-inch square of foundation fabric
- 6 inches of ¼-inch-wide ribbon for center
- Pin back or shoe clip (optional)

what you do

1. Follow the instructions for the Traditional Pansy, page 77, ignoring the references to folding the fabric.

stunning

dahlia

Create a stunning dahlia corsage by arranging individual petals on a shaped foundation.

what you need

- Scissors
- ¼ yard of sheer metallic fabric
- Needle and thread
- Approximately 4-inch square of foundation fabric
- Button
- Pin back (optional)

what you do

1. Cut the fabric into approximately 32 squares, each 3 × 3 inches. Use more or fewer squares depending on your fabric and the size of your foundation. Cut the foundation fabric in a teardrop shape, as in figure 1.

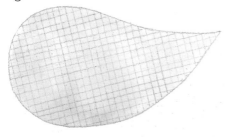

Figure 1

2. Follow the instructions for the basic leaf (page 16), substituting 3-inch squares for 6-inch squares, and folding rather than pressing the folds. Make as many petals as desired.

3. Stitch the petals to the foundation, beginning around the outer edges and working toward the center (figure 2). Stitch the button to the center.

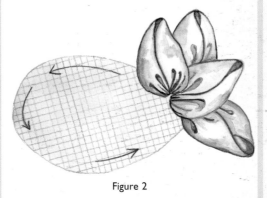

Figure 2

4. Add a pin back if desired.

tip
Folded petals can create distinctly different looks, as you'll see in the next two projects.

81

daffodil

daffodil

An extra fold turns a basic leaf into a daffodil petal. Who knew?

what you need

- 6 squares of fabric, each 6 × 6 inches
- Iron
- Needle and thread
- Approximately 4-inch square of foundation fabric
- 3 × 10-inch rectangle of fabric for center, torn rather than cut
- Scissors
- Pin back (optional)

what you do

1. Follow the instructions for the basic leaf (page 16), steps 1 and 2, for each of the six petals.

2. Fold the points of the base of the triangle to meet at the center; press. (See these folds in the detail above.)

3. Stitch close to the raw edges using a gathering stitch, stringing one petal after another. When all the petals have been stitched, draw up the fabric to gather them into a flat circle; tie off. Stitch the flower to the foundation.

4. Stitch the short ends of the center fabric right sides together, using a running stitch and a ¼-inch seam allowance (making a circle of fabric). Fold this strip in half lengthwise, wrong sides together, and press the fold. Stitch along the fold using a gathering stitch; draw the fabric up tightly; tie off. Stitch to the center of the flower, through all layers. Trim any excess foundation fabric.

5. Add a pin back if desired.

83

loopy flower

You can make these funky flowers larger or smaller by varying the diameter of the cording used to fill your bias tubes.

what you need

- 5 pieces of ⅜-inch corded bias tube, each 5 inches
- Sewing machine with zipper foot
- Needle and thread
- Half a nylon-coil zipper for center

what you do

1. Make corded bias tubes following the instructions on page 20.

2. Fold one corded bias tube in half, positioning the seam at center back. Stitch the cut ends together about ¼ inch from the raw edges to anchor, if desired. Tie off but do not cut the thread. Stitch through the four remaining tubes, pulling each close to the preceeding one (figure 1).

3. Stitch the first and last loops together to form a circle.

4. Make a zipper center following the instructions on page 16; stitch it to the center of the flower.

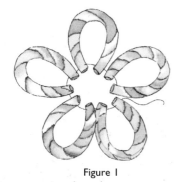

Figure 1

frilly flower

This frilly flower can be subtle or it can shout. Its three concentric rings of petals can be of one, two, or three different colors and/or fabrics, depending on the look you're after.

what you need

- Scissors
- ⅛ yard each of 3 fabrics
- Needle and thread
- Approximately 4-inch square of foundation fabric
- Sparkly button or vintage jewelry for center
- Pin back (optional)

what you do

1. Cut five bias strips that are each 2 × 5 inches from fabric A (outer color). Cut five bias strips that are each 2 × 4 inches from fabric B (middle color). Cut five bias strips that are each 2 × 3 inches from fabric C (inside color). Fold each strip in half, so the 2-inch raw edges meet at the top, and the fold is at the bottom. Cut to curve the top raw edges into a bi-lobed shape.

2. Stitch along the fold of one fabric-A petal, using a gathering stitch (figure 1). Continue stitching remaining fabric-A petals, stringing them all on the same gathering thread. Draw the fabric up to form the petals into a flat circle; tie off (figure 2).

3. Repeat step 2 for fabrics B and C.

4. Stitch the circle of outer petals (fabric A) to the foundation fabric; stitch the middle circle (fabric B) on top of it; stitch the inner circle (fabric C) on top of the middle. Stitch a sparkly button or bijou in the center, through all layers. Trim any excess foundation fabric.

5. Add a pin back if desired.

variation

This bright bloom at the top of the page was made from only two colors of silk.

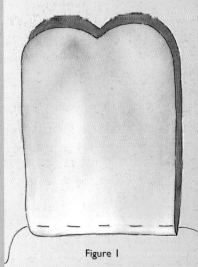

Figure 1

Figure 2

straight strips

Bias-strip flowers can be made up of as many concentric rings of petals as you like, and the petals can be of any shape. This project features straight-cut petals arranged in four rings.

what you need

- Needle and thread
- Approximately ¼ yard of fabric
- Approximately 4-inch square of foundation fabric
- 5 strips of soft netting, each 2 x 3 inches
- Sparkly button or vintage jewelry for center
- Pin back (optional)

what you do

1. Follow the instructions for the Frilly Flower, page 89, steps 1 through 3, but do not curve top edges in step 1.

2. Fold, stitch, and gather the netting as in step 1.

3. Continue with step 4 on page 89, adding the netting on top of the fabric petals before you add the button center.

4. Add a pin back if desired.

tip
If desired, you can add stiffness to soft fabrics with spray starch.

flower field

poppy

Create your own abundant
field of these striking red flowers.

what you need

- 6 strips of red fabric,
  each 3 x 6 inches
- Iron
- Scissors
- Needle and thread
- 3½-inch circle of black fabric for center
- Approximately 4-inch square of
  foundation fabric
- Artificial stamens (or embroidery
  floss) for center
- Pin back (optional)

what you do

1. Press each fabric strip in half
lengthwise, wrong sides together. Cut the
short edges at a 45° angle, beginning at
the folded edge (figure I).

Figure I

2. Position two
strips with their folded
edges to the inside, their corner
edges matching, to create a V shape.
Stitch around the entire V beginning at
the folded edge. Stitch close to the raw
edges using a gathering stitch; see figure I
of the Traditional Pansy, page 77. Gather
the fabric tightly and tie off.

3. Repeat step 2 for the remaining two
pairs of strips.

4. Shape each set of petals with your
fingers. Stitch all three sets to the
foundation, overlapping them to form a
circle. Arrange the stamens in the center
of the flower. Stitch to secure (figure 2).

5. Make a yo-yo for the center (page 43,
step I). Stitch the yo-yo to the
center of the flower, through all
layers. Distribute the stamens
evenly around the yo-yo.

6. Add a pin back if desired.

Figure 2

author's note

The poppy below has
sentimental value for me, as
it was made from some
fabric that my father bought
for me long ago.

93

graphic style